POINT OF DEPARTURE

Poems by

Marina Jaffe

Note

Point of Departure is a collection of poems that reflect my child-hood in Overland Park, Kansas and my travels throughout the U.S., Latin America, and the Middle East. Wherever I was, in Miami or Cairo, in a hospital bed or a mystical vision, images from Kansas and my childhood came to mind and found their way into my poems. As a student at the University of Kansas I looked out into the larger world and saw connections. From Kansas I went to Mexico, then back to Kansas. Throughout my life I have traveled back and forth between Kansas and other places. Many of my poems emerged out of this back and forth movement. As a result, no matter how far from my point of departure I had gone, whether in the back alley of a red light district in Mexico, or a sand dune in the Sinai, Kansas was in my head ready to ground my poems.

April 2012

Editor: Kevin Rabas

Woodley Press
Department of English
Washburn University
1700 SW College Ave.
Topeka, KS 66621

http://www.washburn.edu/reference/woodley-press/

ISBN-13: 978-0-9828752-9-2

Printed by Lightning Source

Library of Congress Control Number: 2012940292

Text design and layout: Pam LeRow
Cover design: Tamar Jaffe
Cover photo: Rita Rosenblit

To contact the author: Send an email to Marinajaffe@gmail.com

Contents

Section IV: What Lies in the Field

Section V: Mustering Prayers

Section VI: Exercises in Looking

Acknowledgements

I gratefully thank my father, Dan Jaffe, my lifelong editor and writing mentor.

For Tamar and Jonathan

The sun! The sun! And all we can become!
And the time ripe for running to the moon!
In the long fields, I leave my father's eye;
And shake the secrets from my deepest bones;
My spirit rises with the rising wind

Theodore Roethke

Though we travel the world over to find the beautiful, we must carry it with us or we find it not.

Ralph Waldo Emerson

Into Mexico

After the Fulbright at KU

Clara prepares to return.
I say, "Be selfish. Stay."
She dreams about Soyapanga,
of her mother, the hairdresser, her father, the shoemaker.

She taps an envelope from them against the table.
She must leave her world of theory, of flirting on the weekends.

We met in Professor Velasco's class,
talked about Claribel Alegria, Roque Dalton.
Tonight we salsa and drink shots of McCormick Vodka.
They go down like grade school stories about the body
she walked past going to school, about the stump
of what was her father's index finger, cut off by the policia.

She is drunk, like her mother's family,
like her father, when he beats her mother.

But tonight she sings their love songs.
In one month she goes back. She has no choice.

For all the choices I have, I say nothing.

The Train from Nuevo Laredo

Across bridges on stilts the train
crossed the northern desert
valleys of Mexico. Water droplets
fell from air vents onto carpet
of the first class car where I sat alone.
The windows framed sloping sand
sprawling across the horizon
encircling us. The conductor,
in a frayed jacket with tarnished buttons
and a collar the color of dried blood,
opened the door to third class seating.
I glimpsed makeshift fans from broken
cardboard, cactus liquor drunk
out of plastic bags with straws,
Toltec girls threading bracelets,
sunlight illuminating floating dust.
I stepped outside between the train cars.
The wind swirled my hair into knots
as I watched pueblito children running
beside the tracks. Orange burned the low sky.
It reflected spirals of Joshua trees
in the glossy heat. I thought I saw an iguana
lap up the sun with the arrow of his tongue.

4

The Singers

Many buses drive along Calle 4 to reach the small beach town Barra de Navidad. Pepe and Marcos wait at a crossing where buses stop. They climb up the steep steps, wait for the driver's nod, then scoot down to the middle of the aisle. Grabbing onto the back of seats, they spread their feet, slightly bend their knees for balance, and begin to sing. Mouths open, eyebrows up, voices in tune. The ride shakes their voices like the suitcases that bump around in the shelves above them. Outside, small circles of dust spin around organ pipe cacti. The boys' ranchera song washes through the bus clanking across the desert. The bus rattles to a stop. Pepe and Marcos scan the passengers. They look for eyes, try to catch them before they fall to the floor, shift to the window or directly ahead. The boys pour down the aisle, collect dull coins, polished coins, bills held between thumb and index, or in fists near knees. Then, they jump out the door and cross the street to catch the bus going back. They stand in the hot afternoon. Dry earth crawls up their toes from the wind.

Accordion Players in Plaza Tapatia

The two boys playing the accordion won't tell anyone their names. Only the taller one will speak. The short one bobs back and forth. He ignores the tourist who tries to talk to him. Both boys are shoeless and dirt-crusted. The short one wanders away. A dusty black strap holds the accordion to his back. The accordion is more than half the niño's size. As he wanders down the street a man with a family points and smiles at the niño. The boy drags along past businessmen, teenage couples, and women with strollers. When he comes to a street vendor selling acrylic paintings he stops. One of the paintings is propped against a tree. The niño stares at its meandering stream, the marshes lined high with waving cattails. He plays his finger on the canvas tracing the water's curves. His finger stops moving. His eyes focus clearly to a spot in between the tall reed plants. He's discovered a boy casting for fish. He stares into the scene, waits for a nibble.

A Sacred Mother

The five-year-old leaves his miniature accordion by a
tree. He climbs on the fountain's ledge, scrunches down,
reaches his hands in, and begins splashing. Then he walks
to the other side and sits down. He kicks his feet through
the water, cooling their bottoms, burnt from walking
barefoot on the sidewalks and streets of Guadalajara.
Glancing up he sees a young mother. She holds a child
about five-years-old in her arms. The young mother's hip
is a throne for her napping child. She stands in front of
the boy and snuggles her cheek into her child's hair. Curls
of light crown her with a glow. The boy recognizes the
young mother. He has always known her— from shrines
on street corners, pictures in the city buses, and statues in
the cathedral. The mother and child's hair are feathers of
light. The boy shoots his hands out of the water toward
the mother and child. When the mother sees his hands
reach for her and her child, she jerks away. She holds her
child tightly and glares at the boy at the fountain. The boy
continues to reach for them.

Jorge

Under the tall building's shadow, Jorge drags his finger
along the stones of the governmental palace until a glare
stops him. In front of him stand two army-green legs and
a bright machine gun. The soldier shouts, "Vete niño!"
The boy scrambles away. He hops on tip toes across the
sidewalk until he reaches a puddle. Then he dashes over
to a fountain, cups his hands, pours water over his head
so it streams over his eyes. The water blurs the world. He
flips his head back shooting water into the air and rubs
his eyes. He spots a tour group near the palace. His hair
spikes wildly as he runs over to them. He circles a man in
a blue jacket who speaks English. The group walks toward
the stone colonial building. He weaves in and out between
the people. He taps on their elbows, tugs on their purses,
yanks on their camera straps. He holds his hand out for
a peso. They all refuse. The crowd enters the palace, and
he hides his ripped shirt and oversized pants among the
khaki shorts and Polo shirts of the visitors. Inside, the
group stops at the foyer of an echoing courtyard. The
boy wanders further inside. He peers up at the balconies
overhead, then sneaks past towering pillars to a wide
staircase. At the top of the stairs he finds Orozco's whirl
of people frescoed on the wall. He takes a seat on the first
step, spreads his arms, lies back on his throne.

Window Washers

They attack the bright red Cavalier and begin scrubbing
the windshield with rags in suds of gray water.
Mosquitoes, Luis lands on the trunk and Rodrigo on
the hood. The sun's glare turns the windshield into a
mirror. Past his own reflection Rodrigo can vaguely see
a screaming face. "Bajate Nino! Get off my car!" the face
says. Rodrigo stares at the man inside. The boy moves his
head so his reflection and the driver's mix. For a moment
he imagines himself inside too. He's the son being driven
to school; he wears a plaid uniform, carries a super hero
lunch box. His mama will kiss him when he comes home
and feed him sugared churros. A loud horn cuts off the
sugar he can taste at the corners of his mouth. Rodrigo
finds himself again on the hot metal hood. Luis hops off
the back and runs over to the man's window. He bangs
on the window asking for a peso or two. The man ignores
him and continues screaming for Rodrigo to get down. The
light turns green. The Cavalier jerks forward, then stops.
Rodrigo slides off the car onto the street. The man takes
off, his tailpipe spouting.

Margarita

Stick it on them when they're not looking, thinks
Margarita. Then passerbys will have to dig up some pesos
for her puffy heart stickers, for stuff like "True Love" and
"You and Me". One senora walks by. Margarita tags her
shoulder with "Think of Me". The senora is out of change.
She tries handing back the sticker. Margarita won't take it.
She reaches for the senora's watch, then her Nikon camera.
"Then give me those." She begins yanking at the senora's
purse. She says again, "Give me those so I can buy some
tacos." The senora keeps walking. Margarita gives up and
snatches "Think of Me" back. She puts it on a man walking
by. He won't have it either and pulls it off, dropping it to
the sidewalk. The heel of the woman behind him smashes
"Think of Me" into the ground.

Felipe

Felipe looks for the moon among the trash and rubble in
the alley behind Independencia Street. He sits on top of a
wooden crate and leans against the walls of Nueva York
Motel. His head falls back so he can look up at the sky
and count the planets on the moonless night. He finds Las
Tres Marias, the Three Marias, in their diagonal line across
the Eastern sky. They remind him of the blinking lights of
the motel. He holds his bag over his mouth and nose and
takes deep breaths. Out of the alley on the curb, women in
spandex miniskirts and black painted eyebrows whistle at
men driving slowly by. One is his mother. The track marks
on her arm have made her forget Felipe. The paper bag
makes Felipe forget her.

Luisa

Luisa sits with her baby sister and knots green and brown thread into diagonal patterns. Woven bracelets line a woolen blanket in front of them. The cloudy afternoon cools into a shiver of rain. The wetness rushes through cobblestone streets of San Cristobal de las Casas as Luisa covers her sister's blue lips. Water falls in bows from the overhang above them. It snaps as it hits the ground beside the girls and splashes Luisa's back. Men with briefcases, grandmothers with bundled children, ladies in high heels all gather underneath the overhang. They crowd in front of Banco America. Luisa calls out to the people escaping the rain, "Dos por un peso! Dos por un peso!" She taps a leg beside her. A mustached man in a tie looks down at the child. Luisa holds up a bracelet. The man holds out a pink candy. Luisa takes the candy and slips it into her mouth. The man looks back out into the streets. Luisa tugs on his leg again, but the man does not move. He straightens his back and crosses his hands. Again the girl pulls on the dark grey pants. The man's eyes do not move from the building across the street. He looks through the storm, hardly blinking.

Alivia

It is twilight in Guadalajara. A young mother walks
through Plaza Tapatia holding the hand of her daughter.
The little girl's ruffled dress is tied with purple ribbons.
Alivia sits against the governor's palace. She curls up
behind her accordion; only her head and arms stick out.
Mother and daughter hurry past Alivia. Alivia looks
away from the ruffles. With her toes she pushes a plastic
container spotted with centavos towards an American
asking questions. Who taught her to play? She points to
herself. Where are her parents? She points to sky, *Arriba*.
She begins to play pulling the instrument in and out. She
won't talk anymore. An older couple pass by and slip ten
pesos into her hand. Alivia holds her hands up. She flashes
ten fingers at the American. She smiles. *Y tu*? Then she
gives the sign: *Chinga tu madre*: fuck your mother.

Jose de Jesus

Jose de Jesus wraps his arms over the back of the park bench. He looks down as the woman in a cream scarf talks to him. She points to his page of stickers and asks how much they cost. Jose holds the metal back of the bench tighter, lifting himself off the ground. The senora keeps asking him about the stickers. Jose peels a blue happy face off. The senora opens her leather purse and pulls out a large silver and gold coin. Jose takes it without looking at her. He turns it over in his hand twice, then puts it in his pocket. A rope tied around his waist holds up his baggy gray pants. The senora stares at the holes in the boy's pants and asks for the boy's father again. Jose points to a rounded fire stove hissing grease. The senora follows his finger. "Oh, that's your father's taco stand?" Jose uses the sheet of stickers as a mask covering his mouth and nose and shakes his head no. He walks away from the woman. The street lights hum. Jose turns the corner and picks up a mango pit impaled on a stick and stuck in a plastic bag. He walks down a winding alley sucking on sweet leftovers.

14

Fernando

While buses make their last ten o'clock rounds, Fernando
circles Plaza de Goyado. He sticks his hands in trash,
searching for aluminum or leftover scraps. A couple strolls
through shuffling pigeons as Fernando struggles to open a
garbage lid he isn't tall enough to reach. I step behind the
garbage can and lift the lid. Fernando looks up at me for a
second and then begins digging. I watch as he rummages
through Styrofoam cups and straws, dirty diapers,
scrunched up paper napkins and a Carlos IV chocolate
wrapper. Nothing looks good on top, so Fernando sticks
his whole arm in. He stands on the tops of his feet. The
metal rim cuts into his underarm. After a moment his arm
stops moving. He pulls it out slowly and opens his hand
in front of his face. A thin layer of dark red wets his palm.
A small grayish blue feather sticks to his thumb. He shakes
his hand wildly and wipes it on the outside of the garbage
can. The feather falls, swaying back and forth down to
the ground. Fernando drops to the sidewalk. Furiously
he scrapes his hand against the pavement, over and over
again, startling a group of pigeons into a gust of flight. He
spits into his palm, then jumps up. He runs off rubbing his
hand on the back of his pants.

Ricardo

Ricardo walks behind a stray dog through the outdoor market in Oaxaca de Juarez. They pass hanging pigs' heads, boxes of avocadoes, crates of guanabanas and flat ribbons of white cheese rolled up and wrapped in plastic. A tomato seller gives a quick swat to the dog's tail to chase it away. Ricardo stares up at a bunch of bananas hanging just out of reach. A vendador sings the bananas' price to a passersby, "Cuatro kilos por un peso!" Ricardo watches women in worn dresses and plastic sandals. The women point, touch, and weigh the fruits and vegetables. They quibble with the vendadores over prices before filling their straw woven bags. Ricardo scratches his head and sweeps out a bug. He leans over a table and reaches for a tomato but pulls his hand back. He turns around to another vegetable booth and taps a guava. He sticks his nose close to it and sniffs. The stray dog passes by again poking his head on the table beside Ricardo. The vendador behind the table shooes them away with a strip of cardboard. The stray scurries down an alley strewn with abandoned crates and garbage. Ricardo sees the dog dig his head in one of the crates. He sees four smashed oranges. Ricardo runs and grabs them. He makes a pouch out of his shirt and drops them in. The dog barks. Ricardo dashes away.

Pedro

Pedro presses his nose crusted with mucous against the
outside window of McDonalds in downtown Guadalajara.
He then runs to the door, but the man with the name tag
meets him there and holds the metal rim of it securely
shut. Pedro bangs on the glass with an open palm. He
makes a fist around the front of his pants and wiggles from
foot to foot. Inside, a woman in a yellow sundress takes
her girl's hand and leads her down the bathroom hallway.
That's where the man had grabbed him. Pedro watches
the mother and daughter disappear behind the shutting
bathroom door. He pushes against the glass door again but
still can't open it. He starts to cry, punches the door then
stumbles away. Shit slides down his leg onto the street.

Juggler

The car fumes fade. Fewer and fewer cars pass the main drag of Avenida Americas. Dusk settles on the glorietas of Guadalajara. The red, blue and silver No. 368 bus stops at the street light crossing of Americas and Lopez Mateos. From the inside of the No. 368 I see a dusty-faced girl stand up. She stumbles in front of the cars. She holds a baby wrapped in a blanket. From the pocket of her sack-like dress she pulls out two mushy oranges. With one hand she begins to juggle. She gets a good rhythm going. Only her left hand moves, not her whole body. The baby goes on napping. Even as she juggles, the girl glances down for a moment at the baby, After about twenty seconds she catches both oranges, puts them back in her pocket, and rushes from car to car. She sticks her open hand through windows asking for change. She knocks on the windows. She ignores No. 368. Its windows are well above her reach. I pound on the outside of the bus, hold out a five peso coin. The light turns green and the bus starts to pull away. The five pesos are still in my hand. I jump to the last seat of the bus. The girl climbs back on the median. She sits Indian style with the baby and waits for the next green light.

Wind of Night

A young Mestiza
sought a vision,
so she traveled to the mountains.
Late at night
she came to a Zapotec pueblo.
She imagined her family
around a husk of fire,
their bodies like
the sun's flames.
She wanted to join them.
Under the arms of the trees
she ate mushrooms.
Lying on her back
she looked up.
The sky wrapped itself around her.
The stars fell
like pearls from a broken necklace.
Soon her flesh
became the soil,
her hair the grass.
Her bones were buried
deep as the roots of the roots
of the Tule tree.
The wind of night
breathed through her.

Theories and Flirtations

Moving Away

Our cedar house looked looted.
My brothers and sisters chatted on the stoop.
We gave each other half warm hugs with half smiles.
The front door was open.
The bare walls almost glowed
where antique family portraits once hung.
Holiday dishes, silver pitchers and crystal glasses
covered the dining room table.
Upstairs mattresses leaned against walls,
their bed frames dismantled.
My parents had divided anniversary gifts from the kids.
My mother got the Aztec calendar,
my father, a hand carved chess set.
Then they split up the books.
I had packed my car tightly with the things
my mother didn't want,
what my father had no room for.
I didn't glance in the rearview mirror
as I drove down the cul-de-sac.
I thought of how skinny my mother's legs had become
of the hollows under my father's eyes.

After the Party

You arrive at four in the morning,
your neck pasted with slick curls
from the sweat of a night's dancing.
The rented townhouse smells like a new heater.
Your feet cramp as you slip off
high heels. Your mother sleeps
in the bed she once shared with your father.

You stand beside the bed in the dark;
she sleeps on the right, her thin wrist
limply hanging off the side like a string.
You can hardly hear her light breathing.
You remember your father's snores
that she claimed pushed her out
of their room to sleep in yours.

You look at her gold-mirrored tray
that sits on your father's heirloom dresser,
searching for the perfume
you always wanted to wear.
You spray it into the air.

You crawl into bed beside her.
Sharing a pillow, your hair and hers
fall into each other like braiding rivers.
Over your shoulder her wrist dangles.
Slowly, you close your eyes, almost asleep,
almost hearing your father's snores.

Marks on the Table

I sit at this table, $20 at a yard sale,
run my finger back and around its dulled edges,
stare at the wood's grain tracing the rings' curvatures.
In the middle of the table three circles,
where the wood is pine-color pale.

My childhood dresser was first my grandfather's
then my brother's. When it reached me
my mother used cream cotton doilies to cover
scratches, nicks, etchings and stains on its cherry top,
the bleached square where my grandfather put his aftershave.

This table belonged to a family with three daughters.
I consider the circles in the middle of the table.
I've looked at the rings long enough to know them all,
and the scratches too. That long one that hops
in jagged lines was a dragged serving plate.

The indented edge at the head of the table:
the father's belt buckle. The marks are like settled coffee
grounds at the bottom of a cup telling your fortune. This line
that looks like an "s" means a lover is hiding something,
this crater-like hole says she will probably be abandoned.

At the Terminal

He walks through the glass doors, and I watch.
Just before, we dragged french fries
through the same glob of ketchup.
Our knees knocked against each other.
We could smell one another's shampoo.
On the other side of translucent walls,

he places on the conveyor belt the yellow backpack
we carried the red peppers and feta home in yesterday.
The front pocket hangs open.
I want to zip it closed.
The bag slips away as it is.
I can longer see its open pocket. Last night's dinner fades.

He talks with security, lifts his arms
while they pass a detector across him.
Through people and reflections
I can see his mouth move.
I imagine what he says. I want to ask him
something unimportant, rub his eyebrows
down even though they're straight.

But those moments have already flipped past.
He opens another glass door, walks through it.
I see a reflection of a reflection, an image
on a screen that comes in and out of focus,
a flickering. But I stand on the other side
until even his reflections disappear,
unfamiliar ones blurred in their place.

Currents in Blue

I.
In your self-portrait the paper's pores become
your pores. Speckles of brown
from the paper's fiber define your skin tone.
The gaze of your pasteled eyes floats
over to your drawing of Miami Beach
on the floor. In it, waves crest
into white strokes like clouds.
Light sighs across blue.

II.
You dug toes into seaweed, searching
for shells so you could rediscover them
in blocks of red clay. We leaned our backs
against each other until darkness
turned the ocean into jagged black,
and red lights from boats misfired on the waves.
While I imagined painting that night into a poem,
You imagined how to sculpt it.

III.
You are in New York now. I listen
to the aria Una Furtive Lagrima
as I study your self-portrait, also your drawing
of waves thrashing into white strokes.
I feel a contraction of the senses
like electrical currents across a vast blue.
like a spasm in the brain,
an anarchy of color in the black sky.

Lost in a Painting

Everything was slanted
in Van Gogh's *The Bedroom.*
When she woke up she felt herself
sliding down into the bed.
She gripped the mattress,
but her fingers lost their hold.
She continued falling
deeper into the canvas,
through the sheet,
past the bed frame
and into the hardwood floor.
Color bled into her skin,
changing its pigment,
like paint mixing on a palette.
Soon her body became streaks
of burnt orange and cadmium yellow.
When she looked out
a brush swirled across her
blending her into the strokes.

Collecting Prayers

Before my sister left for Jerusalem
she collected prayers from the family.
I drew an eye on a piece of paper
and wrote, "Let me see."

When Anna arrived at the Kotel
she slid our prayers
through the cracks.

That night I dreamt I was in a stone cave.
I ran through every passage
until a beam of light struck my eye.

I leapt towards it
and landed in a well,
a funnel with walls aflame.

The gated city, withering and aglow,
rose above me into a dot
which shone white,
then blue
before an eclipse
and the prayers,
all of them,
crackled
into charcoal bits.

Blues in Miami

Point of Departure

On November days in Miami
seagulls squawk and lunch break fishermen
sit in fold up chairs beside the bay.
Green coconuts float between the mangroves.
Every morning when I cross Biscayne
the low sun barely lights a rotting abandoned skiff.

I can't help but think of the Kaw River in fall,
of that two mile stretch between the 6th Street Bridge
heading east out of Lawrence, Kansas and into the woods.
By late October the river is already
a carpet of burgundies with glints of gold rushing;
swirling white blooming around clumps
of mud and leaves caught in driftwood.

The last time I ran along the Kaw,
over wet ash-colored leaves
and twisting roots hidden underneath,
I threw oak and maple branches into the currents
and chased them as far as I could.
Flushed out liquor bottles and muddied shirts
gathered on the banks. From the bridge railing
I dropped dried out seed pods.
They whirled down slowly suspended on caught air
as they became feather propellers.
On the water they were spangles of light until they sank.

Somewhere between North Bay Village and Miami Beach
a wooden post juts out of the water—a landing spot for pelicans.
I drive over the 79th Street causeway, count the sails up,
glimpse reflections of maple leaves and driftwood in the bay.

In the Mangroves

We slipped the skiff into the mangroves
in the middle of the night; you taught me
to lure a line, unhook a fish, and then
I caught my first, a snapper.

Its tail flipped down on the boat's floor
tapping out its end
for longer than we could handle,
so with a quick knife, you cut just below the gills.

We sank into the middle of the boat
next to each other, our legs dangling off one side,
our heads off another. Seven stars dropped across the sky
like the lines we'd thrown into the dark to make our catch.

What I would think of you wasn't the question.
How could we know of what would follow, how quickly
one night in a skiff can take hold and turn, how long
it takes for a life to tap itself out on the bottom of a boat?

Interminable

On my right, a window
overlooks a looped exit
off a highway;
on my left, a drawn curtain;
beside it a machine, a screen
of moving red lines, a tube
connecting it to me;
another tube,
in my arm
leads to a bag
full of liquid,
hanging from a stand.

When I turn
to watch cars
drive the loop,
they seem slow
as the lazy drop
that falls
from the top
of the bag into the tube
stuck in my skin, slow
as the burning drops
seeping, my arms
turning blue and violet.

Pain is slow.
It drips. It leaks
into my eyes. Each car
passes. I count
each drop.
I look to my right,
then to my left.
They look the same.
Both views look the same:
lines, loops
the slow hours.

The Patient

Rolling down the hallway she believed she was the gurney
the orderly pushed; the arms he gripped were hers—
but then she saw another gurney, a body on top,

so she realized she was a body on top of a gurney
passing rooms filled with bodies like limp sheets,
bodies tinted blue, shut eyes, open mouths.

She passed a window overlooking the bay, sun fell through
into lines across the white blanket over her legs. A wet cloth
was placed over her eyes and forehead, all went black,

turning red, the red of her fever, that soaked through, that she left.
She snuck into the other rooms, disconnected heart monitors
and respirators awakening translucent bodies.

Together they headed for the window overlooking the bay
where cruise ships flashed colors into the night.
Gusts of wind slipped under their gowns,

filled them like balloons, carried them away
like puffs. They were blue bulbs
sailing through the salty night to cruise ships.

When they arrived they danced and twirled.
They sipped coral drinks that soothed
collapsed veins. Lights encircled them, whites and yellows.

The ship glided through the bay like an easy breath.
When the nurse took the cloth off her face
she opened her eyes. The cloth was cool and dry.

Breaths Interrupted

For two days, semi-conscious in your bed,
the contraction of your diaphragm left you shuddering.
At eight I believed in miracles— you would recover.
I didn't listen to the nurse who told me to tell you goodbye.
I remember how the smell of rubbing alcohol filled your room.

As I lie in this one, the nurse connects the bag
of antibiotics to my IV. Unconscious, I will not
watch my agony falling drop by drop,
under this white light tinted blue.
I will forget sterile linoleum and cold aluminum.
Now, your sickness gone, mine beginning,
I wonder where you went
once you breathed uninterrupted.

What Lies in the Field

Uno de los Desaparecidos,
One of the Disappeared

Pulling a plastic bag
over someone's head,
winding packing tape around his neck
isn't hard.

Was it done after
smashing his cheekbones
to hurry death by suffocation

or did blows
that collapsed his teeth into his throat
stop the mess of blood

Could one tell who he was
when the body was dumped
to rot in the rain?

You try to piss in front of the toilet,
as if wastes are disposable.

You remember the doctor wanted a urine sample
before removing your appendix.
You were too afraid to pee.

But your father took you
to the bathroom, told you
"Peeing is something men do together."
He began, so you could.

Tonight you vomit,
repeat your father's words.

In an open box outside
his body waits to be claimed.
Rain and wind cleanse his wounds,
drenching yours.

Searching for Four Lines in *El Diaro Chapultapec*

We search the newspaper
for something besides
the bloody sheet
lying in the field,

something like a description
of his birthmark,
or his appendix scar.

We would finger the club
if that would let us
cry enough
to swallow our hearts.

We search for something
that will make us feel worse,
because we have no choice
and we want to.

We feel as he must have
when they took him,
when he understood
the meaning of their laughs.

After the Tsunami

I heard of the tsunami
in bits and pieces,
like scattered debris.
At first they spouted numbers
that reminded me of being a child
and seeing a map of Europe covered with X's
marking camp names and death tolls.
The numbers mounted and I wanted to understand them
as more than bars on a chart or graph.

I watched the surge of pictures, the video
of the wave in its emotionless advance.
The fascination! An apocalyptic force!
It was like seeing God or the devil.

Then I remembered Brueghel's *Fall of Icarus*,
and Auden' response —
I thought of the ploughman
sowing his field in the middle of someone else's disaster.
As I brushed my hair,
purple bodies in the television
reflected in the mirror
like water-soaked raisins.

Malcolm X Park

Gabriel holds up the bottom of his Wizard's jersey
so it's a pouch. He drops beer caps in.
Carlos collects pebbles.
Gabriel marks a checkerboard on the sidewalk with a rock.
The two lay out their pieces.
Short two, they scour the ground and score two more.
Then they argue about who gets to be beer caps.
Gabriel wins because he found the most.
He picks one up, fingers the serrated edge.
When he gets kinged
his men will look like they're wearing crowns.

After the game they find bottles and chase up the stairs
to look over empty and cracking Italian style fountains.
Leaning over the balcony they spot a rat.
Get him! yells Gabriel. Carlos throws his bottle.
It splatters like water off a hot pan. The rat disappears.
Gabriel tosses his bottle way above his head,
watches it spin, flip and career down.
I like to see how it falls, he says.

They look for more bottles,
take turns throwing them down, then run off.
Gabriel circles a marble pedestal
on top an old copper statue,
a fading sea green soldier on a horse.
The marble is tagged "CTU 4 Life".
Gabriel shakes his hand like an imaginary spray can.
He graffities his name
over the plaque that reads Joan of Arc.
Her broken sword's lopped off at the handle.

Emergency Room

She shoves them down, one hand over the other,
as fast as a fireman drawing out a hose.
The first pumps in liquid;
the second sucks out bile and poison.

Tubes go down the throat like needle into a belly.
The first time it's hard to put it in. Grab the skin
between fingers, don't think. Push it through.

It will feel cold as the charcoal drink given the girl
who overdosed, as the aluminum gurney handles
the girl's fathers squeezes onto
before she rolls through the double doors.

Mustering Prayers

Prayer for the Donkey

Passing smoke-filled fishawis,
my foot fell into a ditch
in a beehive alley of Khan el-Khalili.
Had I been an Egyptian donkey carting through
my thirteenth hour, I'd have felt
a whack on my side until I drudged on.
My ankle swelled like the pitas
on the round fired stoves.

Later, in Cairo's Turgemon Bus Terminal,
I wound a scarf tightly
around my injury and waited outside
for a midnight ride to Taba.
A donkey strapped to a wagon hobbled by
not regal as a horse, who will draw tourist smiles
and an occasional stroke to its muzzle.

But who thinks to love the donkey,
with his over-sized ears, ridiculous braying,
obscene black penis? This city donkey
never trots in a field, feels the cushion of mud,
pisses in grass—Who wants to love
the miserable? Look at donkey nostrils, slit
for easier breathing so he will work harder?
Who wraps bandages around a donkey's mangled legs
to cure his limp?

The donkey passes. The call to prayer
blares from a minaret that overlooks
the taxi drivers, newspaper venders,
shoe shiners, and beggars.
I prop up my throbbing ankle,
try to muster a prayer
for all the world's unlovable creatures.

A Holy Moment

My eyes scale the Kotel and the prayers
teetering on top of one another, hanging,
just their ends stuck between stones
made glossy by praying hands.

I say the *Shema* like an intruder, hope
for a holy moment. Through the screened barrier,
I see you on the men's side—a pixeled image of a Jew.

As we leave you fumble something.
I reach for it. You unfold a child's letter
on stationary from the Mount Zion Hotel.
Misspelled words wish for the messiah.

We wander out to the alleys of the Old City
past vegetables stacked like scales on a fish,
past skinned lambs hanging from hooks.

After the Bombing

She drops calla lilies into a square vase.
Their petals curl over themselves.
She thinks of how she folded tissues into bouquets
for him when she was a child.

She puts the vase on the railing ledge of her balcony,
watches rain slide,
like wax dripping down a candle,
into the bowls of the calla lily blossoms.

Slowly, she pushes the vase,
its bottom scratches the railing ledge.
The edge of the vase begins to tip over, until a silence,
then a crash, like snapping fire.

Down below the stalks lie twisted.

Hiking H'mahktesh H'katan

From a cliff of the crater we can see
lines primordial streams carved out
before this was a desert.
Jagged and winding, they lead to one point
where a prism of light shoots through.
Like an orange island, the sun floats up
and spills into the honeycombs of sandstone
and across ridges of flint.

We climb to the bottom of the bowl
and follow a marked trail. The crater floor and walls are a gallery
of zebra stripes, sandy finishes the color of aubergine,
smoky swirls in hardened glass
we often miss seeing, our eyes planted on the ground
gauging our footing against a twisted ankle,
as if we're on a normal path.
But then, because we hear an insect buzz
or feel a creak in the neck, we look up,
see the tremendous well we stand in.
Yes, remember this, we tell ourselves.
Look at the gold and lavender lines
crisscrossing the boulders.
Don't let us forget this moment when
we see where we are again.

The heat won't let us stand still,
so we move on.
fix our eyes down afraid to stumble.
The calls of Pin-Tailed Sandgrouse tumble
around us like loosened pebbles.
Sometimes one of us ventures to the side, discovers crystals
nestled between flaky sheets stacked in steps
or rounded white rock waving like meringue.
We linger in one spot, huff in the heat, traipse along.
Sometimes we march certain as a beetle.

When we reach the canyon's mouth,
we look back. But we cannot see clearly.
The beginning, so hazy and muted.

Crossings

Scaling up a sand dune, powder
pours in and fills your shoes. Once in
you can never get it all out.
Always a few grains lodge themselves
in the fabric, stick under the soles.
And later, when the trek in the wilderness
of camel and kufiyeh, sandstone and granite
is over, something still fixes itself to you,
like the memory of a lost love.

Even so far away, in zigzagging lines
of layered canyons, you trace a felluca
you would tack down the Nile.
You contemplate desert buttes, the cratered
out pockmarks on the arid moonscape,
the ridges separating more and more
from wind storming against them.

And when the black and white
spur-winged plover dips in the air
and flies to the range across,
you look down at the empty carved out
space that separates the two of you
and wonder the quickest way to cross it.

Last Night in the Negev

I lie on this spot of bedrock
not knowing if I'll be back.
The red steps of the cliffs
look like woodpiles set ablaze.
Spiny stems and leaves
razor up through cracks
like the ears of this desert's wild dogs
whining for food.
Red petals dot boulders
like drops of blood.

The wind winds through
this empty carved out river
in swooshes like flash flood waters of another season.

After hours of gusting, a settling—
the desert's meditation.
The sky's last blue glows
around the eyes and mouths of the caves.

A bird I cannot see sings a round of notes, high and crisp.
Then another sings—
a brushing of air.
I must stand, but something in me refuses.
The sun is so low. Time's almost up.

I spot a bird—
his wings, knives,
his vibrato, a squall.
I would capture this place
I cannot return to,
like a firefly inside cupped hands.
But nights make no room for fantasies
that cannot tame claws or teeth.

Exercises in Looking

First View

As the tug pulled the ship through the harbor
its passengers flooded the vessel's decks.
Great Grandma Chaya and her four children
leaned over, facing the new country.

Women waved handkerchiefs
and the flowing white bloomed
like a chrysanthemum garden.
Chaya caught a glimpse of the Statue of Liberty.

The Cossacks had made Chaya a widow.
They galloped through her shtetl
flinging branches of flames into the air.
Fire burst from thatched roofs like a blizzard wind.

As Chaya's ship passed Bedloe's Island her handkerchief
slipped from her fingers like a petal.
And the flames from the statue's torch
smelled like the charred huts of Brailov.

Studies in Gold and Grey

I.
My brother, sister and I
would flirt down the aisles
waiting for Queenie
to pull us beside her
to choose a candy to suck on while we prayed.
She gave me chocolates
in gold wrappers.
I always stared at Queenie's hand—
It quivered the way the men did
in their silent prayers.
She would make me sing
and show her the Hebrew words.

II.
After synagogue my sister and I
stole Mama's slips, hid in our closet
and dressed in the gowns
until Papa found us
and yelled, *get dressed,*
no more playing! The drive
to Shalom Geriatric Center
took twenty minutes.
Papa cried for no reason then.
Mama's voice quivered like Queenie's hand.

III.
Under fluorescent lights Grandpa's skin
looked like white tissue paper.
He was always asleep.
From the head of his bed,
I looked down toward his feet,
at the stiff cotton of his gown.

60

IV.
That evening I slipped into the kitchen
where my parents sat
curled over the table,
talking in grey tones.

I thought of Grandpa—
the yellow that hung over him.

Last Gift

The saddle rests, dust covered
on a cherrywood end table.
It's mine now, for sentiment not sport.
Shadrack, Barbados, and Cavalier
my grandfather's prized horses have been replaced
by brass ornaments, framed drawings, a ceramic horse lamp.

I think it was winter—
Moonboots sliding over snow tracks,
I imagined the red, blue and yellow candle drippings
were flattened gumdrops below our menorah
and I skied in my socks into his hospital room.

I want to remember what he said.
I want to know what I said,
but now I can't even remember his voice,
just that the tops of his cheeks were wet.
No tear drops, just wetness, like water
that settles on the bottom of a newly rinsed glass.

Skin

I dropped grey pebbles
into the fountain outside Menorah Hospital.
I didn't know what gall stones were.
I watched the pebbles waver back and forth
down through the water until they hit bottom.
I imagined pebbles inside the body.

I thought the difference was skin.
Grandpa would press my hand palm down beside his,
then grab a pinch from both of us.
My skin fell back tight around my bones.
Grandpa's stayed loose in a wrinkled peak
that eased back slowly onto his hand.
"Getting ready to let go" he'd say.

After Snowfall

What it was doing in the middle of the walk
leading to our front stoop standing lopsided
and muddied, I don't know. And who
heaped the snow into that ashdump of a hill
littered with dead leaves, used bark from our firewood
for the nose and stuck in uneven kindling branches
for the arms, must've not known
that's not the way to do it,
that you have to warm three clean balls,
one bigger than the next and stack them.
Only carrots are good for the nose,
and the arms need to be the same length.
I scowl at this one, at its abnormalities,
swing my red fist across its head
like a tether ball at recess.
I don't want any more of what's different.

With my boot I kick out chunks
of this snowman that doesn't follow the rules.
I will teach him the meaning of being different.

Meditations of a Daughter

I.
I remember the chapel
where every evening
Papa prayed for his father
as his grandfather would have prayed for his.
I wondered if Papa
really could say the Hebrew
as fast as the old men.
Would God know
or care if he kept up?

II.
One Father's Day I planned my suicide.
That day I hated my father.
We spoke but did not know how.
If I could have, I would have
told him of the meteors
and galaxies I was learning about
in school, of the probabilities
of collisions, how the sun would implode
and suck us all into its heat,
of all the insignificances
we thought significant.
Key in the ignition, looking out
the garage window,
I watched Venus flicker.

III.
My sister Tamar and I watch
the nurse pull back the tape
and lift off my father's bandage.
His shaved stomach
is yellow from iodine
and antibacterial cream.
The five inch incision

right of his navel
is swollen dark pinks and purples.
He can't lift his head
to see the black knots of stitches.

IV.
My father sleeps while I stuff
cabbage leaves with ground lamb
and raisins, fill containers with food,
circle them with plastic wrap and label each.
In four hours my flight will leave.
Michael will arrive from San Francisco
to care for our father.
I finish matching my father's socks,
fill his dresser with folded shirts,
and I have never loved housework so much.
I lie down beside him.

A Mineral in the Dunes

Bicycling down Oregon into California
is an exercise in looking:
At sequoias and barking seals,
at layers and lines stacked
in walls of sawed off mountains,
and always at the gravel just under me.

My tires shoot a spray of sand and dirt
that stick to the back of my calves and ankles,
bits of my life piling up in my thoughts,
pumicing grains that burn.

The roads become lines of memory,
stories of what sent me camping
alone on the border of Guatemala,
of what put me on this bicycle for 1,100 miles.
The stories spin with the tires.

At a vista, a sign tells a history
of water and glaciers snagging volcanic peaks
into bits of rock and gravel
that river torrents
carried to the oceans. Tides and currents
swept wreckage ashore.

I go down to the beach
of dried silica, quartz, feldspar and magnetite.
I trace my toes across these remains:
the light colored weightless crystals
brushed this way and that,
and the heavier darker crystals
not so easily carried away
by the wind that sorts out patterns.
I stand in the middle,
a mineral in the dunes.

Sea Daisies

When I touch its center
floating tubular tentacles
coil around my finger.
They grip at any possibility.

But when the water pulls back
and all is exposed,
the sea anemone shrinks
and draws everything in.
Its green darkens.
It droops like an upside down heart.

It's stuck to this tide pool rock
and from there ensnares what it can,
harpoons what it can
before it dries out and hardens
like one of a thousand shrunken barnacles,
that crunch when I walk over these rocks.

Tonight, if the tide pulls away
the sea daisies will be left
like the translucent yellow egg casings
curled in the pool of flat seaweed and glittering leaves
yards from the surf.

The tide will return soon enough.
Some sleeves of possibility will flow to open water.
Others will hatch between sand and rock.

The Lookdown

Its slim silver tails whips
    when reeled into air. Slowly given line
        until back in water,
    he can be pulled inch by inch out.
        He's a two pound fish on a one pound line.

Coming up again I see
    his narrowed lips
        around the lead ball, the hook I slid
    under the shrimp's spine
        probably half way down his body.

I lie on my stomach
    hands over the ledge,
        dragging him up. For a moment he is still.
    The white underbelly,
        a straight line,
    his sides coined flakes
        of scalloped mica,
    only his gills gasp against oxygen.

His metal eyes twitch deep under clear moist balls,
    and I think of the jack in the bucket,
        how his eyes have dulled,
    how his belly has caved
        to faintly outline his insides.

And beside him—the frozen chum,
    its bloody smell,
        eyes, pale flesh, intestines
    turned into an iced block.

This lookdown is mine now.
    Soon I'll slide my hand

down his head, grasp
him around his back.

A finger's length away, he hangs
when his scaled frame
gives a final snap,
pops the line, tears
back into the water.

www.ingramcontent.com/pod-product-compliance
Lightning Source LLC
Chambersburg PA
CBHW051850040426
42447CB00006B/777